Circle of Snakes
How to END Your Gang Stalking!

Special Thanks

I'd like to thank everyone traveling with me during this strange journey. Especially my family and friends with an extra thanks to my daughter Melanie Torres, Robert Torres, Michael Negron, Janet Puccino, Cecelia Rivera, Jina Puccino, Taylor Guerrieri and the rest of the bunch. Robert, Saige and Aiden. All of the TIs that contributed to my knowledge base and understanding. All the great scientists, authors, beings, entities, the supreme being of course, the universe, the planet, other gods and anyone I left out.

Cover art "Ouroboros" by Robert Torres

Table of Contents

Introduction

Introduction

This manual is written for victims actually experiencing REAL Stalking. Although the focus here is on Government Gang Stalking, it contains information that will be useful to anyone experiencing any type of stalking. I wrote it using concepts and excerpts from my book "Sin Thesis" which is a bit more involved. The goal of this manual is to give anyone a reference for ending this insidious activity. I didn't just suddenly decide to write about stalking, I wrote it because I lived it - it happened to me

Now, beside what I finally did to solve my problems, I have included condensed versions of the ideas that I used against these criminals and my results at the end of this manual. I don't endorse any of you using any of this because you have to decide for yourself what you feel comfortable with doing or not. I am not an attorney, I am an author and a victim of gang stalking telling my TRUE story about what I did and along with some helpful insight. You may decide to use none of it or do nothing at all and that's OK. I lived with it for a long time and only acted the way I felt I had to when I was backed into a corner.

Due to the many questions I receive via email I may continue with future update editions. So after reading this entire manual I encourage you to submit any of your own yet unanswered questions. If you are reading this manual, please buy it. Do not duplicate it or share it because I would like to remain in this battle with you. I for one believe that no one is powerless but there is strength in numbers. We must work together as a united force.

Most people in the world do not care to be anarchists or revolutionists and neither do I. However, many times in life our lots choose us rather than we choose our lots in life. So, when someone wants to make that choice for us, we must act. The system is broken - bent on ruling the world and micro managing the population. It's up to us to free ourselves. - Bobby T

Chapter 1
How it ALL Began

My story starts in New Haven, CT which to me is the gang stalking capitol of the US. I believe that the northeast has an extremely high concentration of these stalker types. The density of the population doesn't help along with the willingness to conform. Nosiness is a huge problem up here with everyone wanting to be in everyone else's business. Also what I believe to be a lot of old school secret society Satan worship going on. New Haven is the home of Yale and the infamous Skull and Bones. Evil just seems to permeate the atmosphere around here.

The story I'm telling is very strange but also very true and I'm sure there are probably much stranger ones. All our stories are different and if I was an international spy then I'm sure my story might be off the charts. In reality most TIs or other stalking victims aren't international spies. Most are just average people who got caught up in this by being chosen randomly in a system gone haywire. For me, I was young, naive and socially conscientious. I wrote some things and was too young to realize that there are things people don't want said. I believe it was at that point I was on the radar of my government.

As I was going through this, I also believed that there was nothing legally I could do until near the end when it got too intense. At that point I had no choice but to do something - anything. What I did after a lot of thought got me results. Now it is beyond important that I tell others going through this about what I did so that they can try to do it too. This isn't going to work for everyone unless you are truly a victim of stalking and are truly committed to ending it intelligently. This is a self-help manual so it is only a tool. You are the most important part in achieving the right results.

I also want you to know that I am against all activities that are secretly being carried out under the umbrella of America upon innocent US citizens. If you have been victimized like me you have been exposed to a shadow government that most people will never believe exists. They blindly go about their lives believing what they're told. If you're like me then you know what our government is actually capable of and will probably wonder why they would want to do this to you? How does a person defend themselves against such tyranny? If you were charged with a crime you could try in court. What if you are never charged because you haven't broken any laws? Well then you have already been convicted having committed no crime and are already in prison. It's a prison for your mind!

Most people don't know this about me but my targeting started very young. When I was 18 and my mind was free I wrote a song about being targeted by the government. It was called "The Awakening" which most people thought was about demons or the devil and in a sense it was. The first lines of The Awakening go: "You reach out your hands and open up your eyes. You think you fool me but I see through your disguise. You are the EVIL that dwells in the night." Way back then I sensed interference – always interference. The record was released on Metal Blade Records out of LA and distributed internationally by Capitol Records. I started getting minor international attention from magazines and airplay, etcetera and my troubles began to intensify. But really I was always writing about what I saw and what I sensed was interference with my life.

Even before that I began noticing strange things occurring around me which is why I wrote The Awakening. It was the start of what would become extremely elaborate street theatre with what seemed like entire staged scenes. Of course like most TIs I was also experiencing the regular theatre too. Most of you will never have to experience the intense stuff which seems almost like Mission Impossible but many of you will. The government is infamous for setting people up with elaborate stings. Rigging motel rooms, bringing the money, the drugs, the actors or whatever and then arresting the target. This happens with politicians or whistle blower types amongst others. It's how they get people out of the way and are able to blame it on them.

My first elaborate scene happened when I was 18 coming home from a show my band performed about 35 miles out of New Haven. There was a roadblock on Route One with lots of cop cars. The State Police were waving traffic through slowly using flashlights. It was supposedly the scene of an accident and there were three bodies covered with blankets in the grass of the center median lined up in a row. All I could see showing was their bare feet facing the road. But they already had toe tags. Thinking it seemed staged I looked back to see a single car with minor damage.

I remember thinking at the time: "Why would bodies be laid out with their bare feet showing already having toe tags?" Where were the shoes? Where was the coroner? Did it have anything to do with the subject matter of my songs? That is what I deduced from it at the very moment I passed. I believed that my songs were the reason and it was a warning. I always noticed little things like this and I knew that they knew I would… So, before that and from that young age that's what I've been going through and it never stopped.

With all of our unique experiences, we are obligated to spread the word to others. We can each play a role whatever that might be. Mine began as a songwriter and continues as a writer. For many of us these are NOT the figments of our imaginations, these are REAL experiences that are occurring.

Chapter 2
Why Does the US Government Target Innocent Citizens and Who are the Gang Stalkers?

"Those who can make you believe absurdities, can make you commit atrocities." ---Voltaire.

Did you ever feel like someone was interfering with everything you do? It doesn't happen to everyone but would you believe that it happens to others? Is it possible that innocent US citizens' lives are being sabotaged? Would you believe that there have been senate investigations into the targeting of innocent US citizens by intelligence groups simply for experimentation? How about other reasons that no one knows about?

Much of this chapter may seem unimportant but knowing stuff is very important as is context. So is of course the history of all of this tyranny. We won't delve too deep, but I tell a story in my last book about my dealings with an attorney and here's a synopsis.

I collected antiques and got arrested for possession of a stolen priceless artifact which made it a felony because of the value. It was missing from the Yale University Art Gallery last seen inventoried in 1963 but it was in fact never reported stolen. Of course my lawyer like any other out to make his job easy told me to return it to Yale and they would drop all the charges. First I reminded him in a very diplomatically and polite way that he worked for me. I then told him that there is a police witness statement on file saying it was given to me as a gift and that the artifact was in fact never reported stolen. I knew all of this because I read the arrest warrant. This meant that the statute of limitations of five years for stolen property expired in 1968. It was no longer Yale's property because it was legally mine and I was too angry about being arrested to be nice.

He then told me that artifacts were exempt from the statute to which I then mentioned that the law only applied to items stolen in World War Two by the NAZIs. In the end I would not relent and threatened to sue for false arrest unless Yale dropped the charges and paid me for the object and my expenses. Yale agreed and we settled out of court for an undisclosed amount of money. As part of the deal I signed an agreement that by accepting the money it would end there.

Now what if I had no knowledge of history or law and went into court like a complete idiot? I didn't know anything about the laws on artifacts or art, or the statutes of limitations but I studied up on it all really quickly.

The moral of this story is that: Reading is fundamental so don't approach anything without background knowledge!

Ok now anyway, the types of people the government targets are a clue as to the why. Protestors, labor organizers, politicians, writers, journalists, whistle blowers, activist and some people (though rarely) may be targeted for legitimate reasons like being foreign spies or terrorists.

Simply put, much of what's going on in the world is one big deception they want kept from the masses. They don't like people who are free thinkers to talk or write about it. They discourage those who don't go along with the program by sabotaging their lives. With whistleblowers it's much simpler to see why. They may have access to some inside information or shady dealings. Idealistic or honest politicians may need nudging to play along with the Washington game. Writers either may have stumbled on to something or just may be too opinionated. So there are many reasons I've mentioned and many more I haven't but you can use your imagination. For many others it's not so clear.

One of my speculations is that there is an evil shadow government that is in control of the US. Now when I say shadow government, I don't mean one that no one knows about. I mean one that is only hidden from the truly blind non-thinkers. It seems only to want to create artificial bad karma for some - a presence of man seeming to be aligned with negative forces. In some cases there may actually be "good or unaware" people being drawn into this as useful tools. At this current point in time however the line between the good and evil seems very fuzzy.

We know that the NSA (National Security Agency) spies on everyone in the US and millions more around the world even though they now say they won't anymore. So, from there the government narrows their focus to millions of people who are flagged for mass data collection. That doesn't mean they aren't still collecting massive amounts of data on everyone else, because they are. Now out of the millions the focus becomes narrowed down to a trickle of many thousands. Many of these then become the TIs (Targeted Individuals). Not every TI ends up being stalked so what causes the shift to stalking?

I've researched this quite a bit and through my own personal experience, unless you are random something about you has to stand out for you to become a stalking target. As I've mentioned, for me I believe it was my writing. At 14 I was writing deep stuff when I should have stuck to writing love poems. But how do we know what things we do are the cause of our targeting? I mean I know now, but while I was young I didn't know there were limits to free speech that extended to opinions.

Unlike many of us there are others who don't yet know they're being targeted because they're just regular people who play by the rules. Suddenly all this bad stuff starts happening to them. Their dog disappears, they are let go from their job, their car gets hit in the parking lot, the house catches fire after being burglarized. Many just chalk it up to bad luck or karma but sometimes it's just not that hard to figure it out. People naively think that things like this don't happen in the US or they just don't know.

Mind you, many people are stalked and it isn't always the government. It doesn't mean it's not happening, it just means that it's not the government doing it. It is however the focus of this manual because they were the source of my troubles and the most EVIL of all EVIL stalking schemes... The people who've sworn an oath to protect our rights are themselves the evildoers. That's the ultimate betrayal. Ok, but a lot of people talk and write about the government, so why isn't it happening to everyone? I mean I don't consider myself any more outspoken than many others I've heard or read in the media. I see postings online that are much more accusatory, over speculative and inflammatory than even me.

So when I first started my research, I never would have if they weren't so relentless. What I found was that everything I was experiencing were being identified as classic gang stalking activities and that I wasn't the only one. What many people don't know is that it's not a secret activity. It isn't even a new activity and in fact it has been going on forever under different names. The operations and the chosen targets themselves of course are kept quiet but the whole program isn't. Everyone in government is aware of what's going on from your local police to the president, to the Supreme Court justices, to the UN...

"The NCVC (National Center for Victims of Crimes) in NYC which keeps statistics, has reported receiving thousands of citizen complaints per month from around the country related to gang stalking. It is a very real problem and everyone involved with the justice system is aware of it.

It's happening to tens of thousands of people. The old cliché that the target is "imagining it" just doesn't work anymore! The only thing now is denying that it's happening to that particular individual. They can't deny it's going on but they can still attempt to discredit people on a case by case basis - which of course they will do in every case. So yes, it's happening to tens of thousands but it's not happening to anyone known? The burden of proof is on you and they will fight you all the way.

I've come to the conclusion that people are hesitant to believe the truth about these programs because they don't want to. The stalkers themselves are "tools" who are otherwise regular Joes and regular Joes are too smart to believe in conspiracy theories. People imagine them walking around in trench coats, sunglasses and hiding behind trees but that's far from the truth. Now in this atmosphere of exaggerated fear of terrorism we have a politicized extremism being whipped up. Everyone has been indoctrinated into domestic spying. "If you see something say something." But what if it's you they are talking about? The new wave of citizen informers are so eager to participate that a mass hysteria seems to have set in around the country. When really we are more likely to be struck by lightning than a foreign terrorist and as some of us know, the real terrorism isn't foreign.

The thing about organized stalking is that those involved can easily deny their involvement. That's the way this whole thing is set up. From its origins plausible deniability was built right in because of its inherent illegality. I'm a fair person, but if you aren't investigating someone for a real crime then leave them alone. The typical target is not being investigated for potential terrorist activity but targeted for ideology. Speech, views, political opinions, associations, involvement in groups that may have gotten attention, civil rights advocates, anything can get you targeted.

Another thing is that those involved with inflicting the suffering consider themselves the "good" people. I consider these people EVIL and I have written extensively about this. Make no mistake about it, this is a military based creation. Those groups not affiliated directly with the military are using the model created by them and the government is often complicit. So, if you think you're going crazy, maybe you as an individual are. I write about this for those who aren't to let them know they aren't alone. It's happened to me and thousands of others…

So, who are these people? My belief is that the US has an overall agenda of nothing less than total global rule. So much of gang stalking then is part of an ongoing experiment because ruling the world necessitates "TOTAL" control. The vast majority will be passively compliant, but for some an individualized strategy is used. For others you have been singled out because of your ideologies. But most are singled out randomly as part of the experiment. Your country has chosen you and for many of you, your lives will be destroyed. For those of you with any doubt you only have to look at our justice system and its treatment of different races or ethnic groups.

The famous Scientist / Philosopher Noam Chomsky said: "The US has criminalized Black life" and they've done it with precision. This is done in the same manner as government stalking. If you are black, in general the system stacks everything against you. Chomsky also said that the war on drugs in the US is a race war blacks are treated different in the entire justice system. If you can imagine yourself being stalked then you know what it means to be black listed. Would our government do this to people? The system is already rigged to do it every day…

The methods have varied with the technology, but tyranny is as old as civilization. Some tyrants of old would pacify the peoples with food or by creating work to give them the appearance of a just state. Over time and evolution - seemingly possessed almost non-human EVIL tyrannical entities befell the 20th century. Inhuman atrocities, war crimes, mass-torture and mass-exterminations have been committed on industrial levels. The objective of globalization in the 21st century is now achieved through terror. They want the power to decide which lives are worthy of existence and which aren't. That's why we are always warring. The government has weighed the lives of those being killed in foreign lands against US military manufacturing jobs. Lives for jobs - pretty simple and in the case of the elite this translate to "Lives for Wealth." For the war machine, war is profitable no matter which side you supply.

Throughout history many world powers have come and gone. Some lasted for several hundred years and the NAZI's Thousand Year Reich lasted 12. The US has been a world power arguably for about 75 years but many believe it won't remain a super power for more than a couple more decades. Many writers, researchers and historians write that the US has modeled itself after NAZI Germany and will start WW3…. Putin said exactly that in a speech. The only option left for the US along with NATO is to fast track the NWO.

"The rest of the world believes that the US poses the greatest threat to the world" --- Huffington World Post—

In their study paper "US Magnetic Weapons and Human Rights" by Peter Philips, Lew Brown and Bridget Thornton (The Sonoma State University Project - Censored Media Freedom Foundation) they write:

"We are in a time of extremism, permanent war, and the unilateral manifestation of ethnocentrism and by a cabal of people in the US government. These power elites have been in operation for decades and are set on nothing less than the total US military domination of the world. They defy the foundational values of the American people to achieve their ends. This is nothing new. The repression of human rights has been present within the US government throughout our history."

I have to agree with this study. The US has positioned itself as the modern day Third Reich desiring nothing less than the military domination of the world! For many of you being targeted, although it may feel like it's all about torturing citizens, there is a much bigger picture. So how did we get to this dark place we find ourselves today?

In my opinion, there seems to be an anxious frustration in certain briefing rooms with our form of government. It allows for too much freedom of the populace and make no mistake, control is what this is all about. This is a war for the next battleground which is the mind. I'm not the first to say this and but of course the control aspect has been going on since the beginning of civilization. Some politicians today want to increase government data collection on citizens.

During the cold war the US learned that the Soviet Union was experimenting with mind control. Of course they couldn't allow the Soviets to get ahead so they had to compete. Also after WW2 the US gave haven to some NAZI scientists and obtained their human research data from the Dachau prison camp.

Using prisoners as test subjects the NAZIs compiled massive amounts of information from experiments which often duplicated real world scenarios. Like how long a pilot could stay alive after being plunged into 40 degree ocean water from a shot down aircraft. But there are other things that our government needed to know like how long it would take to get someone to commit suicide? Could they get someone to commit murder? How can you test unapproved vaccines or medicines? What are the effects of radiation on humans? This was actually tested on soldiers during our first atomic bomb tests in the US that you see on old news reels. The subjects are not selected because they did anything wrong but randomly for training purposes and most never know this is being done to them. Some documented cases ended with the person dying, being killed or committing suicide. It's hard for most people to fathom and you rarely hear or read about it. We falsely believe that human rights violations happen in other countries so it's tough to wrap your mind around.

Trinity atomic tests: The government knowingly exposed unwitting soldiers to radiation - many would later die from cancer.

Of course the US doesn't openly do human experiments here, right? No, we do them SECRETLY… The truth is, interest has shifted to the mind because a more subtle control is required. These new technologies still need test subjects but with possible illness, injury or death being side effects, unwitting citizens are used. When your goal is to control the population of the planet, they aren't necessarily going to go along with it. But what if they didn't know? Timothy L Thomas wrote in the U.S. Army War College Quarterly: "The Mind has no Firewall." Therefore is susceptible to all form of non-detectable intrusions. If your thoughts were altered you wouldn't even know they weren't your thoughts.

In the Military Doctrine paper, "From PSYOPs to Mind War" written by Lieutenant Colonel Michael Aquino, Military Intelligence: he explores using these more subtle approaches like the patented forms of electromagnetic weapons on large scale populations to subdue them psychologically without them being aware of being manipulated. It also lays out our blueprint for the US gang stalking tactics mixed in with NAZI techniques.

Like the SS, the US wants to make it your obligatory duty to watch and inform on your neighbors - with the reward of good citizenship... This works to some degree for isolating the TIs but is of a limited use for the masses. For TIs you must keep in mind that Aquino promotes the idea of convincing the enemy that there is no way they can win before there is even a war. Hence: "PsyOps" psychological warfare or "Mind War" and it doesn't have to be true. Like propaganda, the enemy only has to believe it's true.

So in order to move their agenda forward, the government must create a problem so the people will demand a solution. In the US it's "False Flag Terrorism" and we satisfy this formula by curtailing civil liberties. This allows for more government intrusions into our private lives. After the Boston Bombings they locked down entire neighborhoods and searched every single home. Could you see the ramifications of creating a false flag? The government could then employ a police state under the guise of homeland security.

After 9-11 the DHS created 78 state and regional "Fusion Centers" to gather information on potential terrorists. They do this by enlisting local law enforcement, emergency management, public health and private corporations. They also bring in federal agencies like the FBI and believe it or not the military. Data is then shared throughout the network of participants.

In a report presented in 2012 to the House Permanent Select Committee on Intelligence, the Aspen Institute of Homeland Security Group advises: *"We move away from a defensive position of protecting the country from foreign terror threats. Instead we should focus on becoming a domestic security architecture concentrating on offensive measures on single adversaries."*

This statement translates into "targeting citizens." The report suggests that the mechanisms created in the wake of 9-11 to go after terrorists be refocused to include drug cartels, organized crime and a more all-inclusive approach or what is described vaguely as "emerging adversaries within our borders." It's an anti-terrorist war machine turned into a domestic law enforcement super-tool. What's going on here people, was it all a sham?

What other explanation can there be? This makes perfect sense because in this same two-year investigation they found that these "Fusion Centers'" efforts to compile local intelligence data have not yielded any significant useful information on terrorism. Remember, this whole machine was originally put into motion long ago with these black budget military projects. So it falls right into line with the way it's always been and the way it was always meant to be. The anti-terrorist angle given the track record doesn't hold water.

"Now I can't stress the importance of this paragraph and this entire topic of the DHS enough! It MATTERS that you understand who many of these people really are."

The US currently trains "Terrorism Liaison Officers" (TLOs) to identify potential domestic targets. These TLOs represent their organizations but report directly to the Fusion Centers. TLOs are appointed by their state, local or the civilian companies they work for and go through a 24 to 40 hour federal training. They are made up of police, firemen, paramedics and civilians. Postal, utility, hospitality and transportation workers are also involved. Everyone else is brought in as "civilian collaborators." Friends, family, neighbors, co-workers, police informers are often enlisted to participate and sometimes through deception. They often make up entire stories by telling your family that you are in big trouble or telling your neighbors you are a subject of a criminal investigation. They are then swayed to participate and sworn to secrecy.

Critics of these investigations including civil rights groups are saying that innocent citizens are making the lists. Even worse, there are no safeguards in place for taking someone off. Investigators found people on watch lists for, shoplifting, taking nature photos and even illegal fishing. I know a TI who takes nature photos as he walks. People like this are listed and this is for REAL.

Other accusations are that they are side stepping laws and violating rights by using workers having access to your home to spy without warrants by snooping around. Cable and phone techs, utility workers even the trash collectors going through your trash. Your block watch and neighbors may be keeping tabs on your comings and goings, peeping through your windows even your bus driver may be involved. They use the fear of terrorism as a tool to indoctrinate entire new waves of citizens eager to prove their patriotism. Again, "See Something Say Something" and watch your neighbors like some politicians are preaching. All orchestrated through fear! Fusion centers are also illegally sharing confidential or false information with local police and civilians. This type of big brother policing can never end well and is technically illegal.

The DHS spending on Fusion Centers was estimated at $1.4 billion between 2003 and 2011, the subcommittee said. But the DHS spokesman at the time - Matt Chandler did not respond to a Federal Times request for the 2012 budget. Although the fusion centers are overseen by Homeland Security, they are primarily funded through grants from FEMA (Federal Emergency Management Agency). However DHS can't account for where the money went.

I'll paraphrase here: "Unfortunately, DHS has resisted oversight of these centers. The Department opted not to inform Congress or the public of serious problems plaguing its fusion centers. When we requested documents that would help identify these issues, the Department insisted that they were protected by privilege and confidentiality. It's troubling that these centers designed to help have become such a problem. Instead of strengthening our counterterrorism efforts, they have turned on Americans' civil liberties," said Senator Tom Coburn, who initiated the investigation.

So why is this important? Because to know what's going on around you is important to everything you do. Educate yourself! The Fusion Centers cannot justify how they are spending their money so in order for them to keep asking for more money they have to create phony domestic targets and investigations. People like YOU and ME and other innocent and often unsuspecting citizens. They don't have to accuse us of anything and they don't have to arrest or convict us. They only have to harass the hell out of innocent people to keep themselves working. To justify accepting money they have to show that there is a need for them to get money by having ongoing investigations.

So who are the government gang stalkers? Many are your everyday run of the mill demonically possessed peons working for the GREAT SATAN. The vast majority of the rest are all the citizens desperate to prove they are the "GOOD" people of course! And so now you know that apparently it's everyone but you and me!!! ... I've mentioned the DHS as an example of how this works and how anyone and everyone gets pulled in to being involved. However they aren't the only agency doing this. The shadow government is also continuing with their experiments, projects and so on.

Chapter 3
Techniques, Tactics and Technology – What was Happening to ME

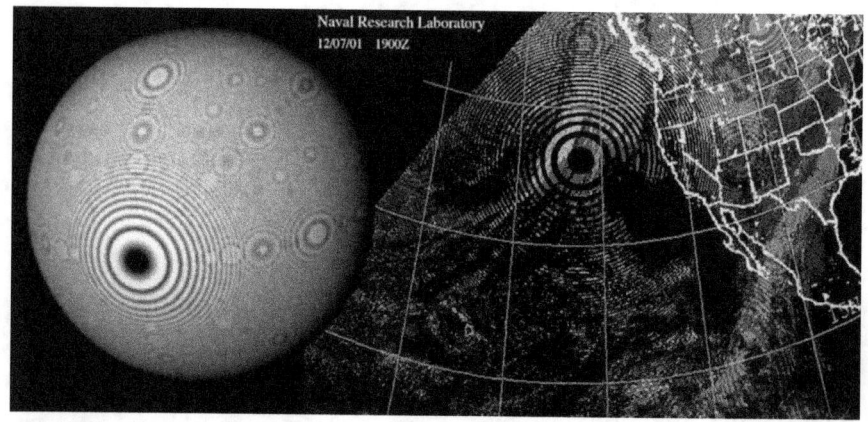

Above: This I suspect was a global psychotronic wave test transmission: *perhaps emitted from HAARP since it is run by the Navy and these images were purged when they found out they had been leaked.*

December 7-8, 2001. GOES-10 Naval Satellite survey of the Pacific region including much of the central US recorded anomalous atmospheric conditions across the full range of frequencies. Both the infrared and visible spectrum measurements revealed an octagonal tiling of concentric circles. The full frequency pulsation was recorded for many hours through the night, over the entire area surveyed by the satellite, the anomalous field most likely encompassed the whole globe for the full duration of the event. Never seen before or since.

Government gang stalking is different than all the other stalking because as I've said: "It represents the ultimate betrayal," not only to the victims, but to the country itself. It isn't only tyranny in the classic sense, it's also traitorous. You may have for some reason been declared an "Enemy of the State," without due process. Another thing that makes it completely different is the overwhelming imbalance of power.

Any of you that aren't familiar with my background should know that I don't live and breathe government conspiracy. I used to be a music reviewer but now write articles for different sites and magazines about everything and anything. Science, religion, spirituality, philosophy, physics, meta-physics, education, politics and one of my favorites, the paranormal. But this EVIL activity happened to me and so I write about it. After reading much of what many of you have gone through in your emails and posts, I'll share with you some of what has gone on with me as insight. In this chapter I'll also include some of what they do and how they go about doing it.

No one of course told me why they were doing these things but I've experienced almost all of the classic TI scenarios. I put much of it together by deduction and some things I've never acknowledged or told anyone even to this day: like the green not so high altitude flares. At least that's what they looked like to me, but I'd see them often mostly when I was alone and anywhere. I was once taking a short cut through the woods because my car was stuck and there was the green flare. This can only be done by someone who knows your whereabouts at all times and wants you to know they know. It's part of their little superior warrior mind game.

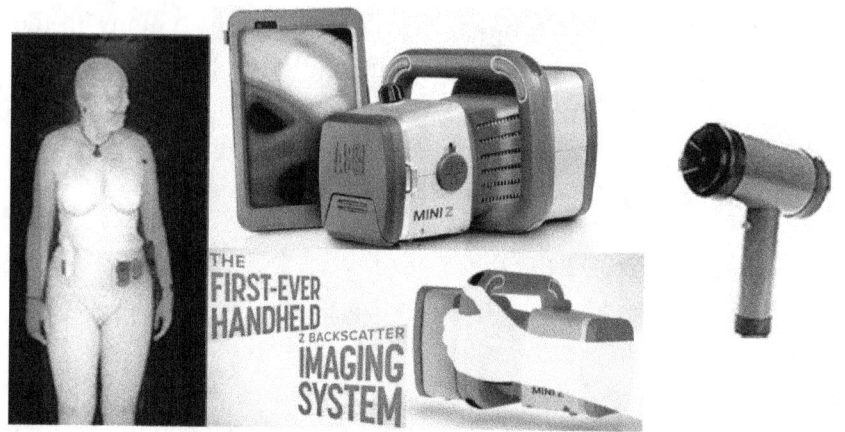

Above left: Image from the backscatter X-ray. The Mini Z handheld backscatter is the same type used in airports and border checkpoints but can be aimed unsuspectingly and can cause cancer if used improperly. Right: Handheld V2K device for direct voice to skull communication.

That tactic was used to let me know that they were always watching. But it also reveals a technique. It means you are somehow most likely transmitting through something you are carrying or wearing. Unless you are truly a TI, most of what goes on would seem far outside your understanding or frame of reference. There is a quote I made up and I put it in my first book: "Most paranoid schizophrenics believe they're being watched and it drives them crazy. I know I'm being watched and could care less." And this my friends is your best defense! Knowledge… Knowing what's going on, keeps you sane. I never told anyone about the green flares until my book. Of course when others saw them too, I just acted as surprised as them.

And another thing I never told anyone but my family about were the military helicopters that were always around but others did notice and mention them. Also to this day I don't believe I told anyone about being sound blasted by an F-18 fighter jet. These are things that the average TI will never experience. For some reason the helicopters became commonplace - the F-18 thrown in was bizarre.

After selling the house, investing the money into my business and losing it because of these people, I was going through some tough times. I moved to New Haven and took a job as a welder to make ends meet. I was living in an apartment provided to me by my work right next door.

The military helicopters had now become part of my regular environment and they were loud. Another part of my routine was going to the New Haven public library to work on my first book. In my research I begin linking the gang stalking stuff to the military but not just because of the constant presence of the helicopters. It was a lot of other reasons too like the entire style, resources and what seemed like a lack of concern for a budget. The research into black-ops like MK-Ultra too became part of the portrait. Then I realized it was all military based including the bizarre happenings.

Now, one day as I'm at home writing on my laptop I hear the loud military helicopter buzzing as usual which you can feel through the ground. This time however I hear this thunderous roar and the entire apartment begins shaking. There it is again after a couple minutes. I go outside to see what it is and it's an F-18 fighter jet directly overhead buzzing my apartment. I mean this was low right above the trees just like the helicopter which was within eyeshot off to the west. This goes on for at least a half hour with the jet having to fly in wide circles. It does this at least ten times right over my apartment. I'm thinking: "They have really gone all out today," It didn't shock me but I was thinking these show-offs are crazy!

But how would they explain what they were doing in New Haven? There is no military airbase nearby but as it turns out they came from Virginia 500 miles away buzzed my house and went back to Virginia. So I wait and watch the news and here's what they say:

Fighter jet flying over Conn. skies
WTNH News
^ | 8/27/09 | Bob Wilson
Posted on **28/08/2009, 09:48:42** by **KosmicKitty**
North Haven (WTNH) - Many people in Connecticut got quite a scare this afternoon when a military fighter jet was spotted flying in circles at a low altitude. News Channel 8 New Haven fielded dozens of phone calls and e-mails from concerned viewers around 4:30pm. "I got nervous, really nervous," said one witness from North Haven. "Back and forth, back and forth for a good 25 minutes and it scared the heck outta the neighborhood." "We were inside the building and you could really hear it and the windows were shaking," said another. The jets were spotted in North Haven, Wallingford, Middletown and Hartford. But what were they doing here?

News Channel 8 went looking for answers. We called the Connecticut Air Guard, the Governor's office and Bradley Airport - no one knew anything about it. We called the FAA and they say it was an F-18 fighter out of Virginia on a legal

training mission but "the military did not notify the FAA" like they normally do.

Get it? The military did "NOT" notify the FAA or anybody else. Another note here is that North Haven is north of the border of New Haven and the jet made wide circles and kept coming back over New Haven and my apartment. I link the military to gang stalking in my research for my book on the public library computer then an F-18 does a training mission over my apartment? The newscast I watched said New Haven and never mentioned the other towns and no one mentioned any military helicopter that was as clear as day from my apartment. I wouldn't have included this story but I found proof of it on-line while writing this manual. Also this from the Hartford Courant Newspaper:

This accidental F-18 fly-by inspired CT, Governor Rell to pen a nastygram to Navy Cmdr. J.J. Cummings at the Oceana Naval Air Station in Virginia Beach, home of the offending fighter jet, according to an August 29, 2009 report in the Hartford Courant by Christine Dempsey and David Owens.

"Witnesses say the jet flew about 100 feet over treetops and performed twisting maneuvers," Rell wrote. "All of this occurred above densely-populated neighborhoods and below radar levels. This represents an incredibly perilous disregard for the safety of our citizens and is absolutely unacceptable."

OK so as bizarre as all this stuff seems to most people to me it was a message they wanted to send and just another day in the life. "We are almighty and can do whatever we want." It could be a coincidence of course – I start writing the military into my book and at that exact same time, an F-18 buzzes my apartment.

Aside from crazy stuff, like most other TIs, I got it all. There was the street theatre and that's where strangers put on a show for you. They usually act like normal people bumping into each other or maybe already in a group where ever you might be in public. Then they start to talk about things that they know will relate to you personally and these are called triggers. Anyone around you not in on it will usually not pick up on the act so it's difficult to prove. Again, this requires knowledge of you which requires coordination through some central source. It all does, it all requires coordination which requires resources and when it crosses town or state lines you can rule out anyone local. Anyway, locals don't usually have budgets for the organized constant surveillance and mental torture of a non- major criminal which describes most TIs.

Using the techniques in this chapter along with modern technology and wave weapons any of the targets privacy can be removed. You can destroy them, their business, their relationships, their jobs. And because everything is done covertly, it's all deniable. If the person doesn't know what's going on, they may think that they were going crazy. If they do know what's going on and tell someone, whoever they tell may think they're going crazy.

There is the use of media… and this gives them away a bit because it means someone can pull big strings. When you have an overwhelming desire to control the masses, it is a natural extension that you would wish to control all forms of media. I use to hang with this one guy who did work for my company. I suspected he might have been planted from the day I met him and how I met him. So I tested this by feeding him phony info. I would just make certain stuff up to see what the effects would be when and if he reported back or called it in. Anyway, every time I would run into him, the same song would play on the radio of my car or any car we were in. One day before I started my car I told him the song that was going to play on the radio. Sure enough, there it was and he said: "How did you know that?" And I said: "Because it's always the same song every time I run into you." He said: "Yeah, but it was the first song. Not like the third song it was the first song." I said, "That's because I'm being watched."

There were the home break-ins where things are moved, or things turned on. I came home one day and in the kitchen area of my home office the ceiling light fixture was on the counter next to the sink and the faucet was running full blast but nothing was taken. There were the car hits, the police harassment, the people following me and others around me. There was the destruction of my business by harassing my clients and customers.

Yes, I started a business out of my home doing mostly internet work but I would often have to meet with local clients and customers. Some of them told me they were pulled over and questioned as soon as they left my house. These were mostly business owners that I was doing custom computer or web work for, graphic design, multimedia, etc... Although most of my business was done online for well-known national companies and chains. Casio, Guitar Center, Peavy, Gibson, The Hard Rock, The House of Blues, Rockhouse, NFL, Ibanez, the Imus Show. I used to be like this computer geek and even set up and taught a specialized computer teaching class for the board of education in my town ...

The harassment got so intense I had to rent a commercial spot in another town, but it continued until my business was destroyed. They want to keep you down. They don't seem to want you to advance beyond a certain point. And most people won't believe that they sabotage businesses while letting others go on without interference. They decide whose business to destroy. I mean they might not care if you succeed as a landscape worker, but they don't want to see some people become successful. This also extends especially to the political arena - Play the game the by their rules or watch your back. Of course they aren't always successful but they can make it as difficult as possible. An anonymous leaked story to the press here or there about a politician? It happens all the time.

Most of these tactics are standard but I've experienced many others that will never be exposed because they are so far beyond believable, like the F-18 fighter jet. What would be the point of caring whether people believe me? It could just be long strings of continuous coincidences. Like the fact that as soon as I linked the military to gang stalking on the library computer an F-18 starts buzzing my house. That never happened before either. See what I mean about coincidence? But it's still only what you can prove.

Much more detail and crazy stuff is in my book "Sin Thesis" but I'm trying to keep this as a short self-help. I experienced electricity cut-offs through entire area blackouts. I'm also sure I was bugged, tapped, things planted in my car... hidden cameras and I suspect electronic attacks, cyber stalking. I was often tailed and pulled over so many times, while almost always having my car and passengers searched. I almost never got a ticket but it discourages friends from associations with you. Several different police departments were in my final written DoJ complaint. The rest of those not in uniform involved were persons unknown to me. I'm sure many were some type of law enforcement and I knew it was all completely connected.

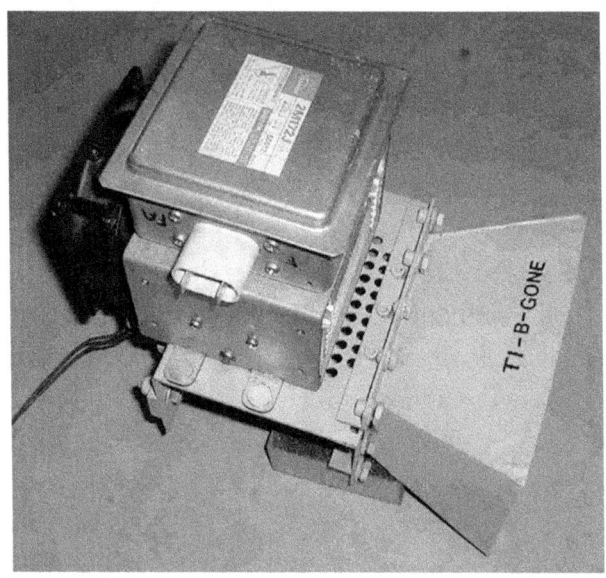

"A Homemade microwave weapon: the magnetron removed from a common high wattage microwave oven mounted to a horn can be placed against a wall in an apartment next door. The victim can be bombarded for prolonged periods right through the walls for example while sleeping. It can also be made by simply removing a microwave door."

Now those are some of the tactics but what type of technology is used? First off, be aware that it is very easy for a non-government group or even a lone stalker to obtain or manufacture some of this technology including homemade wave weapons.

When people mention "Silent Kill" it usually refers to having the target commit suicide. So the tactics are key to the "manipulation of human behavior." These programs use psychological techniques. By repeatedly without cease creating daily nuisances you could create a life of overwhelming stress for the target. As I've mentioned causing them to lose their job, damaging their car, invading their personal space, stealing from their home, taking their mail all these things add up. Normally it would all seem like bad luck. If you could fill someone's life with bad luck and then have the ability to have them audited, you have control of their mental state.

There is another method of silent kill and this is done using high tech wave weaponry. These emit all types of waves including microwaves. They can literally cook you slowly or X-rays can be used which can give you cancer quickly. Like the handheld "Mini Z Backscatter" I mentioned previously. Many others are called psychotronic because with a wavelength at around 8Hz (hertz) they affect your consciousness or "brainwaves." This is because the frequency of your brainwaves are about 8Hz too causing either interference or entrainment. These weapons can be aimed at a target to alter mood, erase memory or kill. These weapons have been documented through investigation as being tested on unassuming US citizens. In 2001, Russian President Vladimir Putin signed into law a bill making it illegal to use weapons of "psycho-tronic influence."

Many countries around the world have on several occasions introduced legislation before the UN to have a global ban on mind (psycho-tronic) weapons but the US has consistently stood in the way. There are also other individuals and groups who are trying to get protective preventative legislation enacted. Including human rights groups and groups like the ACLU, Red Cross, CAHAR... Amongst others who have attempted to pass legislation are The European Parliament and the United Nations Institute for Disarmament Research as part of the UN.

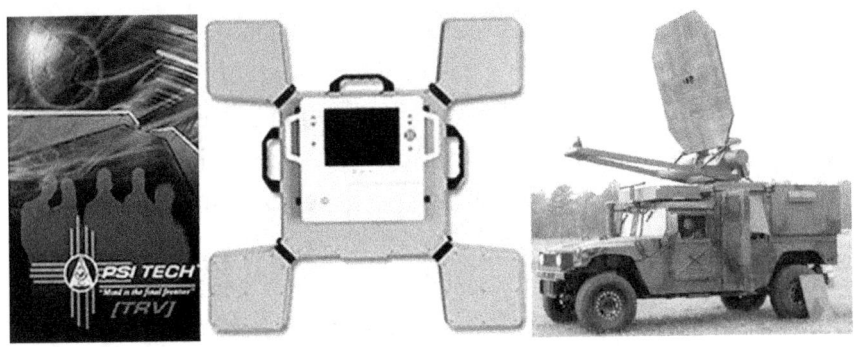

Above Left: PSI TECH webpage logo: They hold the patents to much of this technology. Center: Xavar 800 portable handheld "through wall radar" unfolds for monitoring from outside a room or building. Right through the walls or ceiling. Right: Mounted Military grade EMP - Active Denial System.

As you can probably guess, the US has too much invested in EMP (Electromagnetic Pulse) technology being developed under the guise of non-lethal crowd control. Weaponized versions are available as mounted or even hand held units that can be dialed to the desired frequency and aimed at an individual. Of course military grade can be across the street or across the field. That's because waves will do that! And of course if you know anything about wave technology then you know they can penetrate most barriers.

They also call them silent kill because generally you can't hear, see or feel them and if you are killed in most cases they leave no trace evidence. If high levels of X-rays are used over a short period or low levels over a longer period it simply looks like you got cancer naturally. In my article "Uncovered Photo Evidence of Global Mind Control Experiment?" you can actually see satellite photos of what I believe to be a global wave weapon test. Where would you be able to hide?

There are other technologies and techniques used as well, from high tech to low tech. Car horns to airplanes, helicopters, bugs, taps, cameras, V2K and so on. The goal is to dehumanize you and much of what they use are probably proto-types. The easiest way to find subjects is without consent and that way there are also no law suits, no recourse and if the target is accidentally killed or diagnosed with cancer, there's deniability... Besides, how can you legally experiment on people by bombarding them with high doses of cancer causing X-ray radiation - consent or not?

Dr. Josef Mengele aka "The Angel of Death" at Auschwitz concentration camp, WW2 used humans for all types of insane testing in the name of science. Most of his experiments ended in death because that's how they were designed and hence the name. He tested the limitations of human endurance amongst other things like effects of chemicals, radiation, amputations, transplants and other horrors. Even stitching twins together who of course died! Also he had a fascination with eyes and would have subjects killed just to take their eyes. But unlike our fellow US experiment designers he was a documented demented sadist who enjoyed peoples' sufferings. Here it's top secret... although it's still sadistic and demented.

Chapter 4
Counter Measures and Devices

How do you go about protecting yourself against such a powerful nation as the US's demonically possessed criminal minions? Although some of this is mentioned throughout this manual, there are some things you can do and worth repeating. Knowledge and intelligence are your most valuable tools and really all you'll need. It helps if you are already intelligent but if not, then read more. Remembering and understanding what you read is also important. I myself will read a sentence as many times as it takes until I get it, so concentrate. I also love to learn and believe we can learn something from anyone. "Everyone knows something you don't." Observing is very important too, – be attentive. This is not the same as being nosy because I HATE nosiness. Especially a spouse, sibling, nosey neighbor, etc.... People who spy just to be nosey are really no better than the stalkers.

Awareness: You can observe and read all you want but you must understand what you're reading or looking at. Situational awareness is very important and by this I mean pay attention to everything as it relates to its context. You don't necessarily have to eavesdrop because anything that they want you to see, they are going to make sure you do. Don't go out of your way to see it - that will just have you eavesdropping on strangers. I got to the point where it was more fun to ignore their little subliminal messages like street theatre. You know you can thwart a lot of their little plots just by walking 20 feet away and look in the other direction. It fouls their plans up. I don't get subliminal anyway, so if you want me to get your message it's better if you just tell me to my face. But even if you walk 20 feet away it forces their hand. Do they walk along with you thereby exposing themselves? What if they do and you turn back around? Do they turn around too giving themselves away? You get the picture? Don't make it easy for them, make them work. Never make it easy for them!

These multi-frequency meters below are typical EMF, EMP detectors. Notice that they each have limited ranges and must be capable of detecting the exact frequency you desire. 8Hz is not the same as 8KHz, 8MHz or 8GHz.

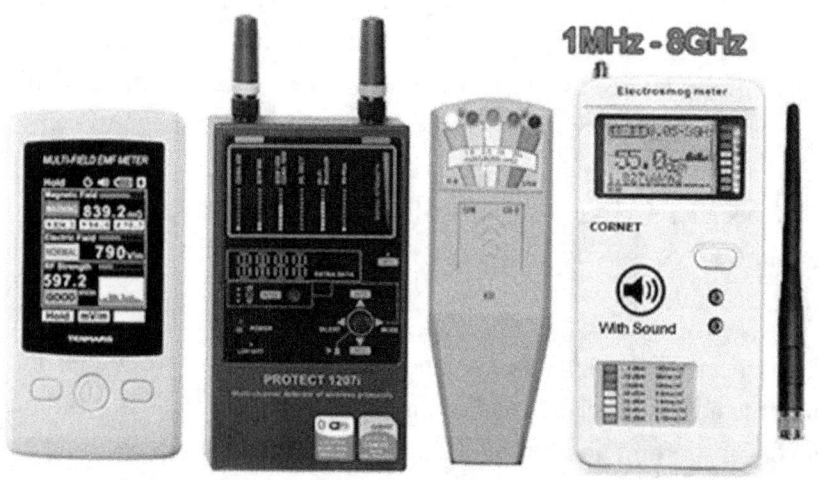

I never bought electronic detectors because my goal was to stop the stalking. I do suspect that I may have been a victim of electronic attack but your options are limited. I don't want to discourage you from doing what you think is necessary because there are situations where detectors might be reasonable. First if you do decide to get a wave detector remember, you may not want anyone to know. If you have concerns about people finding out for any reason, have someone else buy it if possible. I personally don't care what they know or don't know about me because it's just easier for ME.

A situation where a detector might come in handy would be if you suspect electronic wave bombardment. You may not be able to stop or pinpoint the source but you would be able to detect the strongest signal. You would want to of course sleep where you have the weakest signal especially your children if you have any. Or look to someone who knows more about blocking waves. I won't recommend any specific types or brands because I want to keep this manual down in length.

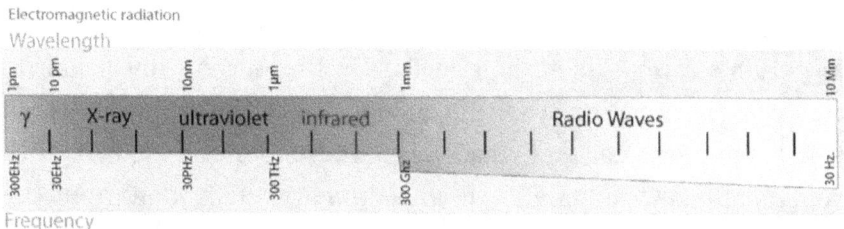

This wave scale above is measured in Hz (hertz) or waves per second from high frequecey on the left (exahertz) above X-ray to low frequency on the right (hertz) human hearing

RF multi-frequency wave detectors are the most common meters. They may be useful for bugs, wireless cameras, etcetera, but you will need a wired camera detector to detect a wired camera as they don't normally emit external RF signals. Also you will need to watch the frequency ranges of any meters you choose to buy. There are many different frequencies and psychotronics transmit way too low for most meters while X-rays are way too high and both require a specialized detector.

One thing I know is that many of you try to shield yourselves from waves and that's fine, do what you feel is necessary. Remember however X-rays cannot be shielded. Not with aluminum foil or any type of foil. Not by building a Faraday cage or mesh or cement or anything. If you want to shield yourself from X-rays, the hospital uses 1-cm lead in the pads they place on you to take medical grade X-rays. Shielding your house will collapse it and X-rays will penetrate 10 feet of cement.

When I first heard of Hugo Chavez contracting cancer along with other Latin American leaders, my very first thought was a military grade X-ray weapon. He was becoming a big problem for the US dream. You can't protect yourself from them and they do exist even in portable form. Again, look at the Backscatter Z Mini handheld and you can imagine what the military has. This emits radiation which can cause cancer. What if I placed one in the next room of your apartment building or used a military grade unit from the house next door? In NYC, national news reported that they drive around in a van equipped with Backscatter Z X-ray. What if I parked it outside your home or across the street from your office and left it on all night bombarding you? If you detect X-rays, move because that means that they are trying to kill you or get experts in there quickly.

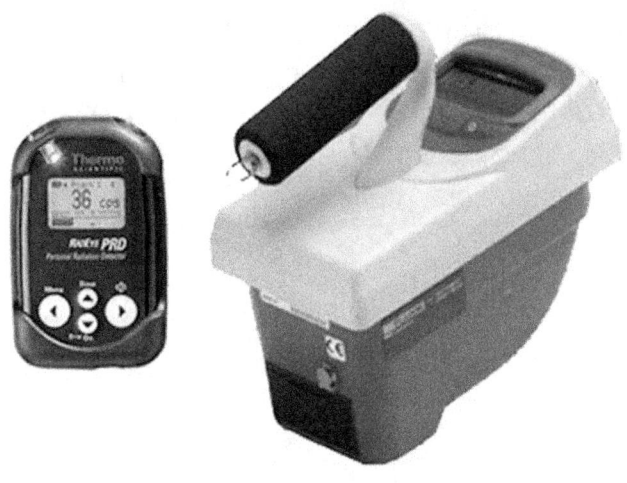

Above: Two X-ray / radiation detectors. The pocket one on the left costs around $2000 and the one on the right is around $3000.

You should never detect X-ray frequencies in your home. There are many common wavelengths you will detect but remember that you also have many devices in your home that give off RF waves. So you may want to get a detector that can pinpoint a signal using a signal strength reading. Also your laptop, TV, cellphone and so on can be used to spy on you. I don't really worry about what people hear but I have tape over my laptop cameras and my phone is never facing me when not in use.

I used to talk to myself a lot or read out loud and I've seen many articles lately that say "Intelligent people talk to themselves." I've always believed that I was being bugged and was always very careful about what I said even in an empty room. It reveals your thinking processes but it's also great for misdirection.

Throughout this manual you will have to just take what you need because your average stalking victim will not identify with what TIs know to be true. Your average TI will not get what TIs like me have been through and TIs like me don't identify with a high priority TI. So pretty much I'm writing only from what I've experienced and my research.

There are many other simple small things you can also do like being careful what you throw in the trash at home or at work, or anywhere.

One of the things that I've run into while writing this manual, I wasn't even going to include was cyber-stalking. A few people online began to attack me personally about my posts in comment sections of websites. The posts were about a political opinion but what they did was made it about me. They began to post things about my book without having read it one posted the cover and said: "Here's what you're dealing with." Then he posted "his book says this and his book says that" and none of what he said is in my book. They went to all my author pages, articles I've written, blogs, everything they could find. Even posting a picture of someone with the same name that wasn't me. This turned into a group of people that seemed to have phony profiles and almost coordinated.

I told them they were slandering and libeling me but they only intensified. I asked one of them why someone would go to all my personal sites for a facebook post about politics? He said he needed to research my past to find things about me and said he hasn't exhausted his resources. Over a discussion on a facebook article comment? That's when I called him an obsessed cyber stalker and told him I was going to write an article using his name and photo about "Cyber Stalkers and Online Predators." He then threatened to sue me and I told him to go ahead. So that's when all of them stopped after hundreds of posts. Threatening to use their names and photos in my "Online Predator" article.

Somehow I believe this is part of an online organized stalking. The internet is full of cyber-stalkers looking to harass, discredit, slander and even worse. Be very careful who you talk to and have an exit strategy. I'm pretty open about being a TI because I write about it. He used one of my articles to try to discredit me until I turned the tables and outed him as a cyber-predator to the group. Have your plan ahead of time to combat these types. Because of this, I plan on writing a second manual dealing with just cyber-stalkers and on-line predators.

Other situations happen on-line when commenting in TI facebook groups. Be aware that there are Agents of Misinformation on every site. They don't want us to participate in groups where we can organize or share ideas. Their intentions may also be to talk so absurd as to discredit the entire group. I've noticed while posting comments to these groups that a perfectly legit conversation suddenly brings someone in to hijack it. With this, you'll have to take notice yourself and decide what an Agent of Misinformation really is. What makes sense to you? Is this person adding or hijacking? Many of them work in multiples as well so one will begin the hijack and others will chime in. That's when I usually just drop out of the conversation.

Often they'll say that there is no such thing as stalking or that it's the work of aliens or the devil. What you believe in is totally up to you. But when someone starts talking about how it's all really the work of some other worldly entities like the devil, to me it's more like misdirection and distraction. I believe government stalking originally stems from black projects. I don't need a hijacker quoting scripture in a conversation about gang stalking telling me that the government has nothing to do with it. Who's manufacturing the wave technology? In my opinion these hijackers are most likely undercover government plants or shills. Don't get me wrong, I do believe in Good vs EVIL influences and even in spirituality but I'm dealing with them in human terms…

Use the phone to contact the FBI, DoJ, etc. Get them to compromise themselves.

A simple way to make the stalkers vulnerable is to use the phone or PC concerning an official complaint and don't forget to also file by mail if that was your original plan. Make sure you back up any communications like documents. Use photo copies and save all correspondence like emails, screenshots or whatever it takes. Never delete your correspondence, save dates, times, extension numbers and get names from everyone even on the phone. Keep it all organized and backed up in triplicate. Don't keep all your back up in the same place either.

Anyway, there wasn't any time in my life since I was around eighteen that I believed my phone wasn't tapped or bugged. So, by using the phone or PC any communications that I had I assumed was being monitored. This means that I was always careful of what I was saying but it also means that any conversations with a federal agency was protected. If it is later found that there was an illegal wiretap or bugging, or PC hack, someone is in a lot of trouble. Listening in on a call you made to the FBI to file a complaint with an illegal wiretap is a federal crime. I would use this to taunt the criminals listening and to protect some of my own conversations. Hacking your computer communications to a federal agency is also a federal crime. Even if you are emailing a congressmen or your lawyer client privilege and so on. You get where I'm going? Pull them into committing as many federal crimes as possible and act dumb about it. Be aware that the police using an illegal wiretap are not immune from committing a federal crime by monitoring these privileged communications.

These little bits of advice or tips will hopefully get you thinking about how to turn your vulnerabilities into useful legal weapons. Don't be afraid to draw the predator to the helpless prey because if they weren't spying they wouldn't know. If you can get your complaint investigated and any wiretaps or trace evidence is found, these periods of communications may be important. Trouble will be had by all involved. But don't get too excited either, because unless you are of high value it may never get to the computer forensics. That stuff is usually reserved for the politicians, whistleblowers, Assange or Snowden types.

Chapter 5
How To End Your Gang Stalking

Before you read these last chapters you should know that I have been partially vindicated due to civil rights arrests being made in my town related to my own personal experiences with targeting. I've included a synopsis again from my first book at the end of this manual. The arrests made world news but it wasn't the whole story as far as I'm concerned. The situation became surreal and blew up with the very odd events that transpired. I tell the backstory from my point of view but you can interpret it any way you want or even as more "coincidence." No matter what you think about what I have to say, it's all true and much of it was written in my first book before it all went down!

Government Gang Stalking is an attack on innocent US citizens by traitors to the United States and the Constitution. If you are a "Targeted Individual" (TI) you are in a battle for your LIFE! Your right to live freely and free from tyranny has been taken from you. Now this may sound anarchistic but realistically it's observational truth telling.

The best advice I can give anyone being gang stalked, I'm probably too late in giving. But that's the way this EVIL manifestation is set up. If you know you're being gang stalked, my advice is to do nothing. This works best if you've figured it out from the onset because it leaves you in the best end position. Knowledge is power and being aware early on affords you the luxury of lucidity. This is your opportunity to secretly and strategically gather information. If you figured it out late, then start using this advice now.

You see, the way they operate is by you doing their job for them through your reactions. So your goal is to turn it around by not being predictable and not making it easy for them. Normally your reactions are made to appear as psychological problems when you start to tell people or seek help from legal or mental health professionals. Once you seek help or start filing complaints you've already begun documenting your own mental illness for them. This can later be used in any event to portray you as schizophrenic, a hypochondriac or trouble maker.

Filing a complaint properly is of course the end game but filing repeatedly and or for frivolities is counterproductive. If you do things right, they won't know they messed up until you file. Their goal is to covertly destroy you while making your daily life miserable. Being aware of this you can often thwart them with counter measures causing them small routine failures. They'll start making mistakes because their intention is for you to be helpless. However in many cases they use average poorly or un-trained citizen cohorts. This weak link can and should be exploited, so be sharp and ready to improvise on the fly.

Be aware that the vast majority involved in the justice system know this is going on but will never acknowledge it. One of the problems is that there's nothing they can do. It is beyond the jurisdiction of any police that aren't in on it. These are powerful forces at work and every cop wants to retire one day. This though can be used to your advantage. No one wants to be involved too deeply when things go wrong. If you can instill enough doubt by causing problems for them, it can wreak havoc with those less committed or less involved. Demons and their minions enjoy attacking helpless prey, so don't be that.

Medieval Painting of Tormented Souls

As I mentioned, the NCVC (National Center for Victims of Crime) in NYC collect statistics on "organized stalking." They receive thousands of complaints about it per month which represents 10% of the total complaints. Police departments around the country also receive thousands of complaints.

Take the case Aaron Alexis who is now infamous as the Navy Yard Shooter. On Sept, 16, 2013 a well-armed Alexis made his way onto a navy base in Washington, DC where he worked for a subcontractor as a computer technician and allegedly killed twelve people. Prior to this however on August 7, 2013 he filed a complaint with the Newport, RI, Police saying that he was a victim of government gang stalking and ELF (Extremely Low Frequency) wave weapons. Anyone who is familiar with these types of weapons and cases give these claims credence. But does this seem like a necessarily satisfactory conclusion? He didn't know where or how to file and these police would not have been able to help. Therefore he felt helpless!

Well then what can be done if anything? First your goal should be to end it without a dark cloud looming. Now as I've mentioned, I know that there are many of you trying to battle the symptoms of the attacks using remedies, devices and gadgets. This manual may not help you with that since it is really for those TIs sincerely looking for a final solution. To do this you must have a well thought out systematic plan.

Let's assume it is the government as in my case. I know based on observations, deductions and thorough research that it was. Then we know they'll be using military based tactics. This doesn't mean it's the military, it could be DHS or any number of covert government entities which are all in collusion. These are just standardized tactics anyway which are the most finely honed. This means that they'll have access to some sophisticated technology. Because of this, you'll have to assume that there isn't anything you can do that can't be monitored. No intelligence agency I know of is more technologically sophisticated than Military Intelligence. Since they work together with the CIA, DHS, black-ops and have access to the satellites in orbit around this planet you can draw all your own conclusions.

Your phone use, computer and the TV channels you watch, your mail, purchases, what you throw in your trash. Everything you do at home, office, vehicle, anywhere you are or travel and walls or locks are not obstacles. So gain some knowledge! Study up, but remember, at the library they will know what you are reading through the computer. Timestamps, IP addresses and even your own computers or laptop IP address request and ID will give you away anywhere you are.

The point here is: never let your guard down and never underestimate them. Assume you can keep no secrets aside from those in your head. Don't assume however that they can't be beat, the best laid plans in the world are often foiled. So even with the most sophisticated technology wars are lost. If you are a target, you have been declared an enemy or a test subject by your government without a hearing. You must know that you can't out think them and you can't out spend them. These government projects have bottomless pockets, technology and some of the world's smartest support personnel.

Your mission then is to be proactive in defending yourself. You do this by compiling data and in order to be effective, you must stay focused. This means not letting down your guard for one second. You must always remain in character as the simple minded easy target… in other words, don't let on.

Now, how do you go about collecting information while at the same time separating reality from fiction? By this I mean reality from delusion! TIs can get so hung up on being defensive we forget that not everyone we meet is part of the conspiracy. It won't really matter anyway if you are going about a law abiding life it's not going to give anyone much ammunition. Even if you have personal illegal habits like a drug problem it won't justify anything they do. Unless they are doing the same thing to everyone in the US with a drug problem then you are still being unlawfully targeted. You have nothing major to hide while they do, so they have something to lose.

As a TI, I often found myself in suspicious situations that I would just roll with. Then later on I'd ask around non-suggestively so as not to appear as though I was fishing. Working things into normal conversations I would see if others had similar experiences. After realizing that I was often the only one going through these things, I noted details. One mistake we make too often is believing that seemingly odd experiences only happen to us. They don't, so be sure.

Let me give you an obvious example. I was getting pulled over constantly, five times in my own driveway and two times in front of my house. Dozens of times in different towns, states, etcetera. So it's easy to conclude that this wasn't normal. I almost never got ticketed leading me to believe that the stops weren't documented. Ask anyone: "How many times do you get pulled over in a year?" The average answer is: "None." The amount of times and locations means that it was being coordinated non-locally. Clues like this can speak volumes…

That's an easy example of it only happening to you, but strange phone calls, street theatre, hit and run dings with your car, strangers always glaring at you. These things seem normal enough but when they occur abnormally frequent, it is NOT typical. These are all bits of information that accumulatively start to paint a picture again straight out of Colonel Michael Aquino's military paper "From PsyOps to Mind War." They must be convincingly compiled in order to be accepted as a whole of proofs if they're to be presented as evidence.

Remember be proactive not reactive. Take photos where you can, jot down license plates along with times, locations, observations, notes, anything and never be obvious about it. However if you were to think anything like me there may be a point to let someone know that you have them in a photo and you may choose to make it appear not to be on purpose. For whatever reason make sure that the things you do are part of a strategy and not impulsive errors.

You want proof, not just your word so be cool about it. Don't hold up your phone like you're taking pictures because they'll alter their tactics. Act oblivious to their presence and pretend you're talking or punching in a number and no one will know. This is the way you have to go about everything. Also things like street theatre are hard to prove so be selective. Use them as examples and be as stealthy as they are. Like I said before, don't give yourself away by buying strange monitoring gear. If you are being attacked by EMF waves you need to end it not monitor it, so save your money unless you are concerned for your health. If you need professional help to build a case and want to prove electronic attack, hire a professional. There are exceptions, but in most cases, a fool is his own lawyer or expert witness!

Just as important, you must know how, where and when to file a complaint and what to include. I filed my very first and only complaint with the DoJ (Department of Justice) in Washington, DC, which brought an end to my stalking. If you choose my route it's important to understand you will be the first to be investigated. Be sure you have clean hands. I did this because I was able to catch on almost immediately that it was government targeting. Not because

I'm smarter than anyone else, but because I don't trust anyone. I don't confide personal goings on with anyone because I don't let people get too close. I'm always suspicious and I don't need a best friend to share personal stories with.

I also don't create problems for myself by causing scenes, confronting people or making petty complaints to police. I methodically evaluate situations and that's how I was able to figure things out early on because I almost never drop my guard to anyone. So I just kept everything quiet and started collecting evidence, like dates, times, suspected incidents, etc…

When I first began to weigh my options, I also knew that I was outmatched. How could I go up against the government and all the resources they have available? I knew that they could be beat, but knew that I couldn't do it. I knew the area police agencies were involved too and you can't fight the law! So who can? Then it hit me, "The law can fight the law!" The trick is finding someone with integrity to care. You may not be able to do that, but you can rely on human traits, like selfishness or self-preservation. Everyone cares about themselves so use that as your leverage.

So, do you complain to internal affairs of the local police department or go above their heads to the chief? The District Attorney, the mayor? Maybe you think: State Police or the FBI? I thought of all these things, but where I live in CT it's not that simple. We have the State-wide Narcotics Taskforce where they all work together. This got me thinking that they were all too close and maybe even go out for drinks or cookouts. Their loyalties may be compromised. I had to file my complaint outside the area and it had to be documented. Remember someone with no ties to the area will look out for themselves. If it's documented that you contacted them and they failed to act when everything goes wrong it's their neck and it's a federal crime.

We know what the results will be if you do nothing but complaining to the wrong people can escalate your troubles. You want to file a complaint where you know it will be documented. You want it on a federal level so there is no confusion that you mean business. You don't want it tainted or surrounded by psychological or domestic histories or other issues. So you've been to psychiatrists, you have prescribed medication, you went to the local police seven times and so on. This lashing out without knowing the source of your stalking never turns out well and is not a good strategy. If you want your complaint to be taken seriously, you must be taken seriously.

But what if your complaint doesn't rise to the level of a federal case? Well hopefully it means you got results and it never escalated. You see, there is a law you will read later in this book that says the police have to guarantee that you are protected from being stalked or from a conspiracy to do so. If you've complained properly and they willfully fail to act then they have become part of that conspiracy by default. This means that they are just as libel to be charged with being participants in whatever happens to you by not doing what they are sworn and obligated to do. That is to protect you! That in itself is a crime and technically an officer committing a crime while on duty rises to the level of a federal crime. "Acting Under the Color of Law." Also later in this book.

When filing, your complaint must be concise, professional and written intelligently which is not the same as "well written." When I filed with the DoJ, the form asked for simple details and a brief description of my complaint. File using any provided forms and don't attach or mail unsolicited materials. Don't send anything unless you are contacted and asked to. Even when you do submit evidence, don't send incoherent ramblings, piles of notes, sketches, pictures etcetera. Send exactly what they require and the rest available upon request. If everything is kept professional including your attitude, that's the way you should expect to be treated. If you don't know how to do things professionally then get help.

Now you should know that I didn't seek or retain help from anyone but I did massive amounts of reading and especially on laws and the history of all of this stuff – like past cases and results. Don't attempt to do what I've done unless you are extremely confident. I've had substantial interactions with the courts, contracts and what have you. I've been writing all of my own contracts since my nightclub performing days way back when and also took a writing class. This means that I know how to word legal documents. However I've never been foolish enough to go to court without a lawyer as my mouthpiece. It's just all part of the game and it's their game.

Luckily there are classes at most community colleges to learn how to write contracts. Usually part of a business course and very often stand alone. Online also you can learn because writing specifically for legal documents is different than just a writing course.

Although this manual is supposed to offer solutions, I can't take into account every scenario or even everything that happened to me. The intensity and extent of the abuse will depend on who you are and why it's happening. Are you a whistleblower, a journalist, writer, someone with inside information, test subject, random?

Some things you should look out for are like oddly running into old acquaintances. And people you meet or situations that may seem random are often not by chance, friends of friends, strange coincidences, etc... These things have happened to me so many times that they defied all statistical laws. Don't let people know what you're up to or the inner workings of your mind. Remember, only allow people to see what you want them to. Think of everything you do or don't do as feeding information or creating a story. Now I don't expect that many of you can naturally act out these roles. However, these are extraordinary circumstances and may require extraordinary measures. You are a citizen often being subjected to military tactics as a civilian by your government or others. Have you had military or counter intelligence training?

Of course if you have nothing to hide, then just try to be yourself. But how is an innocent target supposed to react to constant attacks? If I told you everything that has happened to me, it goes far beyond the pale into the realm of unbelievable. Some of it is in earlier parts of this manual some more in depth stuff is in my last book and some I have still never told anyone. As with anything, just be smart about it. If you think you've experienced everything that the perpetrators have to offer, I can assure you that I've experienced more than most of you and then some. The things I have told you in this book are the things necessary to get the information across. The things I can tell absolutely no one about are things most people can't fathom.

Does that mean there's no hope if you did everything wrong? I have done enough research to know that most of you did, but mostly because we are all normal humans. When we get harassed, we call the police. We think we're going crazy we seek help. Even when we put it together we're too naive or gullible. We look for people to confide in who may actually be in on it. We bought into reporting bad cops to internal affairs. We believe we can tell all our problems to friends we meet and so on.

Predictability is exactly what this system is built on. Wars are fought and won based on being able to anticipate your enemy's next move. Manipulating them to make that move is part of the art of war. If you did do everything wrong you may still be able to do something to end it by starting now. You might still be able to recall or document enough incidents that have happened where you may be able to prove something's been going on. In many cases these stalkers don't cover their tracks well because there is no need. The system is based on people being clueless easy targets. REAL ROCK SOLID evidence is your best friend, accusations without it can bring you to a halt very quickly.

OK, we could go on forever with scenario after scenario but everything comes to an end. This after all is only a guide and everyone may not get the same results. If you have any questions, most can be answered by reading this entire manual. You could always email me but keep it short and only email me if you've purchased this manual and have read it in its entirety. Some of your questions may be used for the 2nd edition if there is enough interest without using your names of course.

Chapter 6
Collecting Evidence and Filing a Complaint

Ok, so now after reading all of the information contained here you've decided you need to do something about what you believe is going on with you.

First here's a tip: File your case solo and not in a class action. I'm not saying you can't be a party to a class action down the line, but you must know who you're filing with. There are many people claiming to be victims of stalking who aren't for one reason or another. Like attention getters, the mentally unstable (hypochondriacs, schizophrenics, etc…) and very often the perps (perpetrators of the stalking) themselves. As far as the perps, their mission is to interfere in any way possible including discrediting. So when filing jointly in a small group or a class action, you are often judged by the weakest link. You may truly be a victim, but in your joint complaint the next guy may not be. Get your solo problems resolved first or you may risk your own case by being connected to the other one.

Another tip: Keep your mouth shut! Don't let anyone know about anything you are doing as far as building a case. Now, did I do that? No, I didn't adhere to my own advice because I had a different strategy but we're all different. When I told people around me almost everyone believed me! There were too many people around me while these things were going on that witnessed a lot of the craziness, so they believed the rest. For many of you telling even your families can be disastrous. In the end when and if you get results, you can let it all out and the only proof you'll need is the arrests... or restraining orders which will vindicate you.

What type of evidence?

So, the first thing you will need to do is collect some evidence and but how do you go about doing that? Well, you will first have to decide what type of complaint you are going to file. I can guide you through the process, but I can't do it for you. You will have to put in your own work and if you pay attention to what I write you will realize that with a little brain power and a plan it isn't really that hard.

In my case I believed there were no specific laws covering gang stalking but I knew there were laws covering peripheral crimes and so those are what I focused on. You will do the same thing to build a successful argument for your case. This means you will pick apart exactly what's happening to you and list in your mind specific things that are considered crimes. That's where you will put your energies. Who is responsible and what solid evidence do you have or what evidence do you know for sure you can get? By documenting multiple smaller crimes a criminal pattern may emerge linking the crimes together which will elevate the charges.

In my case since I believed that there were police participating I decided to concentrate my efforts on them. Particularly, "Acting Under the Guise of Law" by conspiring to target me. By targeting I mean that I am being singled out to be treated differently than anyone else that may be doing the same thing. In many cases just to pick on me and working in concert with others to stalk me. So for instance, if you follow my car every day 365 days a year and watch for a traffic violation of course I'm going to get more than one ticket a year. Failure to use a blinker, not coming to a complete stop at a stop sign (rolling stop), going through a yellow light or parking on a line in an almost completely empty parking lot. I've gotten tickets for all of these. And believe me, I couldn't believe it either. Even worse most of the time I was pulled over for nothing and not given an explanation or a ticket.

"Acting Under the Color of Law" means that you are committing a crime while on duty but this also applies to anyone in law enforcement. Plus it may also apply to them if they are acting in the same capacity while off duty. It's a federal crime for anyone acting under "color of law" willfully to deprive or conspire to deprive a person of a right protected by the Constitution or U.S. law. It is also a crime to knowingly allow them to be harmed or stalked by others. Especially if you've filed a complaint and something happens because they failed to act. Since it is a federal crime it means that you file this complaint directly with the DoJ or the FBI. **DO NOT** file with the State Police or local law enforcement. Do NOT even mention it to anyone other than federal authorities.

So in your case it may be different. There may be many little nuisance crimes like getting your car keyed, broken window, vandalism. You may be experiencing major acts like burglaries, getting major car damage, your pet killed. This list could be endless and of course for many of the nuisance crimes I myself didn't file complaints because I was focused on different evidence for the big picture. But for many of you documenting these little things may be of importance because it may never escalate beyond that. The only way to escalate it is by proving a link or pattern between the crimes as I mentioned or somehow involving the police for not doing their job if it's a major crime. Talk to someone in the FBI if it gets to that point.

Putting in the time.

In most cases you are going to have to convince the police to do their jobs and this is going to be part of the strategy you will use to get results.

How you interact with police and others involved with the justice system means the difference between them choosing to do their jobs or not. I have almost never hired a lawyer who just did his job. I always had to remind them that they worked for me. In both cases as with the police, I was never unprepared. There was never a time where I said: "Just do your job." I made it as easy for them to do their job as possible by looking up case law myself and handing it to the attorney or citing it verbally to the police. I always did this in a partnership fashion and most often friendly manner. "We are going to get results together" and almost never condescending. A smart client makes an attorney look smart and a smart, friendly interaction with police is very wise. A very smart client also leads them to believe that they better be on their toes. It's very easy for you to turn that intellect in their direction. How many attorneys or cops lose their jobs because they underestimated a client? Malpractice can also be a crime. It's up to you to tell a lawyer what you want and it's not your job to ask them what you should do. They are a tool or a mouthpiece for you.

There's a scenario where your car got scratched for the seventh time and police did nothing but you have pictures. Plus your house got broken into and they still haven't done anything. They didn't even take fingerprints but in most cases, it isn't directly because of you. To many it's just routine and to others it is because of you but most of the time it's just standard procedure for that particular department. I don't know of any police department that is going to take fingerprints for a simple low dollar value car or home break-in.

So if you call the police and with this foreknowledge simply pretend to be understanding and let them know that you want it documented. Don't go out of character and start talking about "crazy stalking." They'll write that down many times and comment that you seemed delusional, schizophrenic or obnoxious. Just build your case by getting everything documented. It's not about your frustration or anger, it's about goals. And although it's not in your best interest to mention it, after the seventh little crime that you get documented others might start to mention it or at least wonder what's going on? Just don't ever even fake one car scratch or anything else because you will jeopardize the entire credibility of your complaint.

After the first incident, some of you should think about being proactive and maybe set up your own surveillance equipment. And when you catch someone on camera, think about how important it is for you to go to the police. If they are in your home, of course it becomes a priority but if they key your car or throw a rock through a garage window, does it have to be reported that day? You can look up the laws in your state but you have time to report a crime. You may want to wait to catch them on camera a second time or a third.

One time doesn't prove they did it more than once and if you report it they may be more careful. Two times proves that they are targeting you. Remember, you want them to make mistakes. I won't tell you what you should do but you might want to run things through your head a bit before doing anything.

This is what I did with the police. I waited until they pulled me over 30 times at least until I filed a federal complaint because once or twice wasn't going to prove anything. And I never let on what my intention was but if the conspirators left me alone things would have been different. Finally, how could they explain pulling me over so many times? I knew they wouldn't be able to.

So, learn the laws about specific things that are happening to you, what you can prove and where you go to report it. But if you are trying to or need to prove a pattern as in stalking or a conspiracy as in more than one person being involved, then bear with the low level stuff and document it. In the end you build 10 scratches to your car, three broken windows, a back door busted and so on. Use your own judgment. Do you want someone arrested for breaking your window of which nothing will happen to them or do you want someone arrested for stalking?

Remember, you want the biggest bang and the biggest bang is getting the maximum charges filed. Do you want to elevate the charges from a misdemeanor to a felony or from local to federal? Getting the charges elevated pretty much means "game over" and it sends a clear message. It's too easy for someone to blow off a vandalism charge. How easy is it for someone to blow off a felony or a federal arrest? So read up on all the laws in your state on what constitutes harassment, stalking or conspiracy and use that brain to draw in your predator. Just make sure that the trap is set and the law is on your side. Don't go outside of the law to build your case. I did things I won't mention to draw them in that may be too unethical for most so I won't mention them. And I'm not speaking about drawing in violent or potentially violent offenders. Again use your head and your own judgment and be careful.

Federal laws are also very important for you to know because there are many nuances to these laws that you can utilize for your plan. If anyone in the justice system is involved, go to the FBI or DoJ website and read up on these laws. The overview for "Acting Under the Color of Law" is only one page. "Color of law" simply means that the person is using authority given to him or her by a local, state, or federal government agency. By depriving me or interfering with my right to live free and pursue my happiness they were misusing that authority. I've also posted it at the end of this manual.

I didn't worry much about any crimes that fell outside the boundaries of my plan for filing because all of these peripheral things can be discussed with whomever contacts you. Clutter never really helps and a "to the point" synopsis will be more effective than a thirty page complaint. Unless of course they ask for one!

Breach the wall and it will send the rest running to distance themselves from the coming collapse. Remember, deniability works right alongside compartmentalization because when someone goes down they are easily made to seem like rogues or bad apples.

Some more of what I did and the final outcome

One of the first things I learned from the stalkers was how to act just like they do. When in public they play the roles of complete strangers who have no interest in you. So I pretended I was oblivious to my surrounding including their presence. I acted intimidated by the police and like I didn't want any trouble. I pretended always like I didn't want to make waves. By doing this they see you as clueless weak prey and it draws them in but more importantly, they let their guard down. They get bolder and start to get sloppy because you are their helpless victim. In the end the weak prey act is turned around into the unforgiving predator when they are served.

This is why I always complied (they love compliance) and humbled myself to their authority. "Yes officer, no officer, I'm sorry officer" that kind of thing. I often questioned them but did it politely. I would say: "Officer, can I ask you a question?" and believe it or not, I was told to shut up more than once. I complied of course but when I was afforded the opportunity I would ask why I was being pulled over?

I once asked if maybe I fit the description of someone who just fled the scene of a crime? Another time I asked a senior officer from the town I lived why I was constantly being harassed? He said: "Do you want me to put you in the back seat and end it for you right now?" I could go on with incident after incident. But unbeknownst to me in this incident my PDA video somehow turned on without me noticing. So my niece standing in my driveway watched as the cop pulled away and said: "Your shirt pocket is blinking." I looked down to see the rapidly flashing light of my PDA through the pocket. Believe it or not my PDA accidentally caught the entire conversation between me and the cop and he must have seen it blinking too.

After this encounter with a senior officer in my town all hope was dashed that it could be just rogue subordinates. It was then I knew that in my town they were all aware of what was going on from the rookies to the top. So from then on I just stopped asking why. Once a cop in that same town even knocked at the door of my house and said my headlights to my car were on. I went out to turn them off and saw that they weren't on and my car was locked. I had those headlights that popped up from the hood with motors and I said to the officer that my lights aren't on. He said that was two hours ago. I pivoted dead on the spot and walked away because they couldn't be in the down position having been left on. It was a LIE!!!

If this isn't happening to you because they would never, it's more likely they choose to use different tactics. Very famous and infamous people have been harassed in this manner.

Once you have done everything by this manual and file, be patient because it may take a while. With me I immediately noticed a heavy amount of increased surveillance but it was a long time (two years) before the first arrests. This I believe was a two pronged approach and one was to see if I was truly being harassed the way I said and two because I believe I was also being investigated. They don't want to go out of their way for someone involved in criminal activity.

People have said to me, aren't you afraid about speaking out? It's too late for me, because I already put a lot of my story into a book. Plus with this being my second book, I haven't stopped writing about these evil traitorous people. So be visible and be more trouble for them than it's worth. Sign petitions, write to your congressperson, write an article, a book, join groups, protest, but whatever you do, don't be silent and don't lie down. Fight back but do it smart. Keep the conversation going and stay visible and help others by spreading the word.

Chapter 7
The Final Outcome and a NEW Beginning

Now here you will have to draw your own conclusions but from my point of view I've already drawn mine. Although I have been as open as possible in this manual, there are many things even to this day I can't reveal. In this final chapter I give you results but I was very careful throughout the manual to tell you what I could without telling you some things I did. I was telling people for a few years how this was going to turn out. Not many people believed me when I told them that some of these cops were going to go to prison for what they were doing to me. Much of my tactics to bait them may have been unscrupulous, but they weren't illegal. People said I must be doing something wrong for this to be going on. I told people to think about it. Would someone who is doing something criminal be contacting the FBI? In the end, was I the one put in prison or were the real criminals sent to prison?

I told you how I filed a complaint with the Department of Justice on their website. They had forms made just for that, that you could fill out online. I filled out a civil rights complaint form for "Acting Under the Color of Law." It asked all my personal info and contact. Where it asked for the Police Department, Town/City, Officer's name, I put "several different towns in my area" and wrote officer's name as "many different officers." Where it asks for a brief description, I gave a brief description of what was going on including being pulled over five times in my driveway and dozens more in area towns.

This was a tumultuous period during which I was moving myself and business between several towns. I didn't hear back from them, so I made a follow up call a few weeks later and explained my case to whoever answered the phone there referring to my online complaint. After listening to my brief story, the nice man put me on hold. When the phone picked up it said "US Attorney General's office, we can't answer your call right now so please leave a message." I gave all of my identifying information, contact and again referred back to my online complaint. Almost immediately I noticed many different strange cars following me and I figured that a DoJ investigation had begun.

The US Attorney General's office is in Washington, DC and it is the pinnacle of police power in the US. The head of the DoJ holds this office. So the man from the FBI almost seemed like he was expecting my call when he transferred me. It was all just weird, that's all.

Since that time, my town of East Haven, CT where I now live and the city adjacent to my town New Haven have both made world news. In both towns officers were arrested for patterns of civil rights abuses in accordance with a little known and rarely used conspiracy law. US Code Title 18 Section 241 which you can read at the end of this manual you will also find referenced on many gang stalking sights along with the East Haven story. Everything I tell you on here is searchable in Google or Bing. My name will not be attached to it as you will read but the interesting part is I began writing about all of it in my last book before any of the arrests. They just refuse to admit that there is a shadow government gang stalking program.

Continuing on - in New Haven where I was living during the time of my complaint, the police department was raided by the FBI. Three officers were arrested after a sting operation. The head of narcotics was arrested for stealing money and planting drugs on countless citizens. He was 64 years old and about to retire when he stole $27,500 planted by the FBI. He was sentenced to 38 months in prison and was ordered to pay $45,000 in fines and penalties. The other two officers were also sentenced to prison and fined. The police chief resigned and they disbanded the entire narcotics squad. 30 officers from that squad left the force completely. It was since replaced with a task force under control of the FBI and the State Police.

What happened in both towns was something straight out of an action movie. In New Haven the head of narcotics noticed what he thought was a strange car following him to work. He called ahead and the car was swarmed by New Haven Police. Turns out it was the FBI and then they ascended upon the police department with warrants in force.

In the town of East Haven where I live now, the FBI, State Police and US Marshals along with locals cordoned off entire neighborhoods to conduct pre-dawn arrests of the police at their homes. They went in with FBI Swat and submachine guns ordering the cops to the floor at different locations. They of course terrified the families but it seems a little poetic justice came calling.

The town where I live now which was also included in my original complaint has been covered by just about every major news outlet in the country. It's been on CNN, NBC, UNIVISION, ABC, FOX, CBS, MSNBC, The New York Times, Huffington Post, the Associated Press and many other media outlets around the world. In my tiny little town of East Haven, the US Department of Justice arrested four officers including their supervisor for civil rights violations amongst other charges. They were convicted of targeting Latin citizens and businesses and trying to drive them out of business by targeting their customers for illegal traffic stops. They were actually videotaped by a local priest who was also arrested. The police chief was allowed to retire after calls for his resignation and arrest. The four officers received prison sentences after trials ranging from about a year for cooperating to the most time of 5 years for one officer. Most of the force of 50 officers have since left. My town as of this writing has 18 cops left and they must now wear uniform cameras after an agreement with the Department of Justice. The town is also under a DoJ compliance agreement which they signed.

Although my business would technically fall under the heading of a Latin owned business, it's a misdirection to me just another cover story. My hassles began way before my business began. Plus now, who compensates me for what they did to my business? I'm not a party to this current complaint and my business is defunct. It's not enough that these cops simply serve time, what about the years and investment someone puts into a business? By the way, two of these officers in my town and the major players in New Haven were some that were directly responsible for my harassment complaint. Plus what about the embarrassment I felt when I was telling people around me that this was going on and some thought I was imagining it? And why does it take so many complaints for anyone to do anything?

Being partially vindicated I should be partially satisfied, but it goes way deeper because the way the arrests happened, the stalking as always wasn't acknowledge directly. When you research these cases you find in the final FBI documents that the officers reported to others that were mentioned only as conspirators but weren't arrested. They in turn reported to the chief also named as a conspirator. In my town there were calls for the mayor to resign too… The union reps were named as knowing and covering up. This is just smoke, mirrors and the sacrificial lambs of the system of deniability. Notice that both towns got rid of the cops harassing me and both for reasons having nothing to do with harassing me. I see this only as the system covering its own tracks. Everyone is in on it and these guys are simply the fall guys.

It's like place the blame on the local authorities and use misdirection. Yes they did commit the crimes they're accused of, but they weren't alone and this is obviously in my opinion systemic. In my case, they obviously weren't the ones arranging the car accidents. Plus the pull overs happened in other towns and other states as well. These just happen to be the two towns I lived when filing. The exact same things that are happening here are happening all over the country to others. I know for a fact that these arrests are not coincidental to my DoJ complaint.

The dates of when the investigations started coincide exactly to the dates I filed with the DoJ and I know this from news reports. The fact that the cops that got prison were directly responsible for harassing me is another coincidence? Also there are many things I still can't reveal about how I did things because it will give too much of an insight to how I think. The problem with that is TIs or stalking victims won't be the only ones reading this book.

I did things that may be considered dirty deeds to entrap the snakes but nothing was illegal, just dirty play like they do. They could never have been drawn in by anything I was doing if they weren't illegally stalking me because they wouldn't know. And you never know when I may need to use certain plots again. Also many other strange and behind the scenes happenings occurred that I may have to use again.

In the case that happened with the head of the New Haven Police Narcotics Squad, the New Haven Register newspaper reported that he had over 700 informers on the streets when he was caught. That could give you an idea of what TIs are up against.

Chapter 8
Samples and Miscellaneous

Samples and miscellaneous related to my case but your forms and findings may vary. Everything you need can be found online once you've determined your avenue of procedure.

In East Haven the cops were charged under - US Code Title 18 Section 241 (from the DoJ website below)

Section 241 of Title 18 is the civil rights conspiracy statute. Section 241 makes it unlawful for two or more persons to agree together to injure, threaten, or intimidate a person in any state, territory or district in the free exercise or enjoyment of any right or privilege secured to him/her by the Constitution or the laws of the Unites States, (or because of his/her having exercised the same). Unlike most conspiracy statutes, Section 241 does not require that one of the conspirators commit an overt act prior to the conspiracy becoming a crime.

The offense is punishable by a range of imprisonment up to a life term or the death penalty, depending upon the circumstances of the crime, and the resulting injury, if any.

TITLE 18, U.S.C., SECTION 241

If two or more persons conspire to injure, oppress, threaten, or intimidate any person in any State, Territory, Commonwealth, Possession, or District in the free exercise or enjoyment of any right or privilege secured to him by the Constitution or laws of the United States, or because of his having so exercised the same;...

They shall be fined under this title or imprisoned not more than ten years, or both; and if death results from the acts committed in violation of this section or if such acts include kidnapping or an attempt to kidnap, aggravated sexual abuse or an attempt to commit aggravated sexual abuse, or an attempt to kill, they shall be fined under this title or imprisoned for any term of years or for life, or both, or may be sentenced to death.

Color of Law (from the DoJ website below)

Section 242 of Title 18 makes it a crime for a person acting under color of any law to willfully deprive a person of a right or privilege protected by the Constitution or laws of the United States.

For the purpose of Section 242, acts under "color of law" include acts not only done by federal, state, or local officials within the their lawful authority, but also acts done beyond the bounds of that official's lawful authority, if the acts are done while the official is purporting to or pretending to act in the performance of his/her official duties. Persons acting under color of law within the meaning of this statute include police officers, prisons guards and other law enforcement officials, as well as judges, care providers in public health facilities, and others who are acting as public officials. It is not necessary that the crime be motivated by animus toward the race, color, religion, sex, handicap, familial status or national origin of the victim.

The offense is punishable by a range of imprisonment up to a life term, or the death penalty, depending upon the circumstances of the crime, and the resulting injury, if any.

TITLE 18, U.S.C., SECTION 242

Whoever, under color of any law, statute, ordinance, regulation, or custom, willfully subjects any person in any State, Territory, Commonwealth, Possession, or District to the deprivation of any rights, privileges, or immunities secured or protected by the Constitution or laws of the United States, ... shall be fined under this title or imprisoned not more than one year, or both; and if bodily injury results from the acts committed in violation of this section or if such acts include the use, attempted use, or threatened use of a dangerous weapon, explosives, or fire, shall be fined under this title or imprisoned not more than ten years, or both; and if death results from the acts committed in violation of this section or if such acts include kidnaping or an attempt to kidnap, aggravated sexual abuse, or an attempt to commit aggravated sexual abuse, or an attempt to kill, shall be fined under this title, or imprisoned for any term of years or for life, or both, or may be sentenced to death.

Color of Law (from the FBI website below)

U.S. law enforcement officers and other officials like judges, prosecutors, and security guards have been given tremendous power by local, state, and federal government agencies—authority they must have to enforce the law and ensure justice in our country. These powers include the authority to detain and arrest suspects, to search and seize property, to bring criminal charges, to make rulings in court, and to use deadly force in certain situations.

Preventing abuse of this authority, however, is equally necessary to the health of our nation's democracy. That's why it's a federal crime for anyone acting under "color of law" to willfully deprive or conspire to deprive a person of a right protected by the Constitution or U.S. law. "Color of law" simply means the person is using authority given to him or her by a local, state, or federal government agency.

The FBI is the lead federal agency for investigating color of law abuses, which include acts carried out by government officials operating both within and beyond the limits of their lawful authority. Off-duty conduct may be covered if the perpetrator asserted his or her official status in some way.

In 2014, FBI cases led to 72 indictments for color of law violations.

- Excessive force;
- Sexual assaults;
- False arrest and fabrication of evidence;
- Deprivation of property; and
- Failure to keep from harm.

Excessive force: In making arrests, maintaining order, and defending life, law enforcement officers are allowed to use whatever force is "reasonably" necessary. The breadth and scope of the use of force is vast—from just the physical presence of the officer...to the use of deadly force. Violations of federal law occur when it can be shown that the force used was willfully "unreasonable" or "excessive."

Sexual assaults by officials acting under color of law can happen in jails, during traffic stops, or in other settings where officials might use their position of authority to coerce an individual into sexual compliance. The compliance is generally gained because of a threat of an official action against the person if he or she doesn't comply.

False arrest and fabrication of evidence: The Fourth Amendment of the U.S. Constitution guarantees the right against unreasonable searches or seizures. A law enforcement official using authority provided under the color of law is allowed to stop individuals and, under certain circumstances, to search them and retain their property. It is in the abuse of that discretionary power—such as an unlawful detention or illegal confiscation of property—that a violation of a person's civil rights may occur.

Fabricating evidence against or falsely arresting an individual also violates the color of law statute, taking away the person's rights of due process and unreasonable seizure. In the case of deprivation of property, the color of law statute would be violated by unlawfully obtaining or maintaining a person's property, which oversteps or misapplies the official's authority.

The Fourteenth Amendment secures the right to due process; the Eighth Amendment prohibits the use of cruel and unusual punishment. During an arrest or detention, these rights can be violated by the use of force amounting to punishment (summary judgment). The person accused of a crime must be allowed the opportunity to have a trial and should not be subjected to punishment without having been afforded the opportunity of the legal process.

Failure to keep from harm: The public counts on its law enforcement officials to protect local communities. If it's shown that an official willfully failed to keep an individual from harm, that official could be in violation of the color of law statute.

In 2014, FBI cases lead to 72 indictments for violating color of law.

Filing a Complaint

To file a color of law complaint, contact your local FBI office by telephone, in writing, or in person. The following information should be provided:

- All identifying information for the victim(s);
- As much identifying information as possible regarding the subject(s), including position, rank, and agency employed;
- Date and time of incident;
- Location of incident;
- Names, addresses, and telephone numbers of any witness(es);
- A complete chronology of events; and
- Any report numbers and charges with respect to the incident.

You may also contact the United States Attorney's Office in your district or send a written complaint to:

Assistant Attorney General
Civil Rights Division
Criminal Section
950 Pennsylvania Avenue, Northwest
Washington, DC 20530

FBI investigations vary in length. Once our investigation is complete, we forward the findings to the U.S. Attorney's Office within the local jurisdiction and to the U.S. Department of Justice in Washington, D.C., which decide whether or not to proceed toward prosecution and handle any prosecutions that follow.

Civil Applications

While the FBI does not investigate civil violations, Title 42, U.S.C., Section 14141 makes it unlawful for state or local law enforcement agencies to allow officers to engage in a pattern or practice of conduct that deprives persons of rights protected by the Constitution or U.S. laws. This law, commonly referred to as the Police Misconduct Statute, gives the Department of Justice authority to seek civil remedies in cases where law enforcement agencies have policies or practices that foster a pattern of misconduct by employees. This action is directed against an agency, not against individual officers. The types of issues which may initiate a pattern and practice investigation include:

- Lack of supervision/monitoring of officers' actions;
- Lack of justification or reporting by officers on incidents involving the use of force;
- Lack of, or improper training of, officers; and
- Citizen complaint processes that treat complainants as adversaries.

Under Title 42, U.S.C., Section 1997, the Department of Justice has the ability to initiate civil actions against mental hospitals, retardation facilities, jails, prisons, nursing homes, and juvenile detention facilities when there are allegations of systemic derivations of the constitutional rights of institutionalized persons.

Report Civil Rights Violations

Form **COL**	**Violation Warning** **Denial of Rights Under Color of Law**	
	▶ Violation Warning—18 U.S.C. §242; 18 U.S.C. §245; 42 U.S.C. §1983	

Name and address of Citizen

Name and address of Notice Recipient

Citizen's statement

I certify that the forgoing information stated here is true and correct.
Citizen's signature

▶

Date ▶

Legal Notice and Warning

Federal law provides that it is a crime to violate the Rights of a citizen under the color-of-law. You can be arrested for this crime and you can also be held personally liable for civil damages.

Attempting to cause a person to do something by telling that person that such action is required by law, when it is not required by law, may be a felony.

18 USC §242 provides that whoever, under color of any law, statute, ordinance, regulation, or custom, willfully subjects any person in any State, Territory, Commonwealth, Possession, or District to the deprivation of any rights, privileges, or immunities secured or protected by the Constitution or laws of the United States ... shall be fined under this title or imprisoned not more than one year, or both.

18 USC §245 provided that Whoever, whether or not acting under color of law, intimidates or interferes with any person from participating in or enjoying any benefit, service, privilege, program, facility, or activity provided or administered by the United States; [or] applying for or enjoying employment, or any perquisite thereof, by any agency of the United States; shall be fined under this title, or imprisoned not more than one year, or both.

42 USC §1983 provides that every person who, under color of any statute, ordinance, regulation, custom, or usage, of any State or Territory or the District of Columbia, subjects, or causes to be subjected, any citizen of the United States or other person within the jurisdiction thereof to the deprivation of any rights, privileges, or immunities secured by the Constitution and laws, shall be liable to the party injured in an action at law, suit in equity, or other proper proceeding for redress.

Warning, you may be in violation of Federal Law and persisting with your demand may lead to your arrest and/or civil damages! Also understand that the law provides that you can be held personally responsible and liable, as well as your company or agency.

You are advised to cease and desist with your demand and to seek *personal* legal counsel if you do not understand the law.

Notice of Service:

I, _____ certify that I personally delivered this notice to above named recipient and address on _____ at _____.

Public Domain—Privacy Form COL(01)

Resources

Aquino Michael / Col. Paul E. Vallely in 1980, From PsyOps to Mind War: The Psychology of Victory.

DoJ: http://www.justice.gov/

FBI: https://www.fbi.gov/

Hartford Courant Newpaper

New Haven Register Newspaper

The King James Bible.

Mr. Timothy L. Thomas: Foreign Military Studies Office, Fort Leavenworth, KS. 1998

The New York Times

Torres Robert: Sin Thesis: 2014

WTNH TV New Haven

attempt to verify and add a citation on any further resources used for this book.

Author Bio:

Bobby Towers is one of the author's pen names for listing "Circle of Snakes" separately from other projects. He is a self-described paranormal magnet who is also a published songwriter of "Then There Was Rock" and "The Awakening." Towers has done work for many well-known national US companies as a freelance. He has also worked as a magazine editor, technical, music and content writer, consultant, web designer, promotions, computer multimedia technical production and the list goes on. Currently Towers is working on his next book and writes as a freelance contributor for many online sites and offline magazines.

Please help me stay informed and current with my efforts in this community by connecting with me. Unlike my other projects, this one has to be through word of mouth. By you spreading the word and with enough interest I can continue. Thanks! Bobby T

Contact:

I really enjoy hearing from you, my email is: rttowers3@gmail.com or friend me at: https://www.facebook.com/robert.torres.94064176 Also connect through: https://about.me/towers3